THE COUNTRY GUITAR STYLE OF
✦ OF ✦
CHARLIE MONROE

BASED ON THE 1936 - 1938
BLUEBIRD RECORDINGS BY THE MONROE BROTHERS

BY
JOSEPH WEIDLICH

ISBN: 978-1-57424-249-2
SAN 683-8022

Cover by James Creative Group

Copyright © 2009 CENTERSTREAM Publishing, LLC
P.O. Box 17878 - Anaheim Hills, CA 92817

www.centerstream-usa.com

BROWN COUNTY JAMBOREE

BEAN BLOSSOM - IND. - ON HIGHWAY 135

SUN. NOV. 6

2 SHOWS 3:00 & 8:00 P. M. D. S.T.

W S M GRAND OLE OPRY

PRESENTS - IN PERSON

BILL MONROE

BLUE GRASS BOYS

EXTRA ADDED ATTRACTION

CHARLIE MONROE

Popular RCA Victor Recording Star

TABLE OF CONTENTS

INTRODUCTION
THE MONROE BROTHERS

One of the more popular country "brother" and/or "duo" acts in the mid to late 1930s were The Monroe Brothers, i.e., Bill (on mandolin and tenor vocal) and Charlie (lead vocal and rhythm guitar). Other well known duos of that period included the Morris Brothers, the Blue Sky Boys, the Delmore Brothers, etc., just to name a few.

Bill and Charlie Monroe were familiar with the recordings made by the better known string bands from the late 1920s, such as Charlie Poole and His North Carolina Ramblers, Gid Tanner and His Skillet Lickers, and the Carter Family, as well as more "commercial" artists as Vernon Dalhart and Bradley Kincaid. The Monroe Brothers arranged some of those songs to fit the then popular mandolin-and-guitar duo style.

By the early 1930s the Monroe families had relocated from their farms in rural Kentucky to the greater Chicago metropolitan area working in local oil refineries and factories. Bill and Charlie Monroe, avid square dancers, were hired by Chicago radio station WLS to occasionally tour with their live square dances shows; eventually, their abilities as musicians was noticed and they were able to eventually quit their day jobs, hired by a patent medicine company that sponsored regional live daily radio broadcasts promoting its products in the Midwest. This was common practice in the new developing era of radio broadcasting. For instance, Flatt & Scruggs would later be sponsored by The Martha White Company on that company's segment of WSM's Grand Old Opry radio broadcasts, as well as their weekly television program sponsored by Martha White in the late 1950s and early 1960s.

At that time live local radio broadcasts allowed its' more popular performers to promote their upcoming regional concerts, which was their main source of income. The sponsors also rotated their "talent pool" from radio station to radio station every few months or so. While playing on radio broadcasts, now transplanted to the Carolinas, the Monroe Brothers growing popularity among Southern listeners led Bluebird Records (a division of RCA Victor, devoted to the recording and distribution of country and blues artists) to sign them to an exclusive recording contract in 1936. It was during that time that they developed an emphasis on recording up-tempo and gospel songs allowing Bill to show off his evolving personal approach to playing mandolin. Over the next three years and six recording sessions they recorded 60 songs for Bluebird, a "baker's dozen" of which eventually became "instant classics" in the bluegrass repertoire such as "Roll In My Sweet Baby's Arms", "My Long Journey Home" and "Roll On, Buddy".

By 1938 the Monroe Brothers decided that it was in their best interests -- personally, professionally and financially -- to discontinue performing as a duo. For instance, Charlie Monroe often complained that while many of their recordings were being sold the Brothers weren't receiving very much money in kind from RCA/Bluebird. In fact, performer royalties from record sales at that time were virtually non-existent (for instance, it is estimated the Monroe Brothers received 1/8 of one cent for each 78rpm sold, split between them!). Obviously, large volume sales benefitted only the record and music publishing companies, not the performers who, more often than not, simply received a "flat fee" for each song recorded (and were grateful to receive it in that post-Depression recovering economic climate). After the split, each went on to form their own groups; after several false starts Bill's group eventually was billed as "Bill Monroe and the Blue Grass Boys."

Let's now look more closely at Charlie Monroe's guitar performance style (who used just his thumb and index finger) at those Bluebird sessions, as it is a transitional style from the string band style to the newer, faster pre-bluegrass bass line note style. This 2-finger style was used by many early bluegrass guitarists, including Lester Flatt and Carter Stanley.

CHARLIE MONROE BACKUP TECHNIQUES

Charlie Monroe's rhythm guitar style is loosely based on the traditional string band "boom-chick" patterns that are outlined in my book "Old-Time Country Guitar Backup Basics" (based on commercial recordings of the 1920s and early 1930s), in particular those of Riley Puckett (guitarist with Gid Tanner and His Skillet Lickers), who seemed to use more bass lines based on chord outlines and chromatic scale fragments than many of his contemporaries.

I need to make note of the fact that Charlie Monroe suffered from the same affliction that Henry Whitter (of Grayson & Whitter) and Riley Puckett often did: getting lost in their backup patterns, thus faking their way through until they found a chord change where they could continue their rehearsed patterns. In the case of the Monroe Brothers part of that problem can be traced to the simple fact that they didn't use a consistent count-off leading to the downbeat of a song, particularly when using pickup notes; thus, it was not unusual for Charlie Monroe to take two or three measures to get in sync with Bill. Another complication is that around the middle of a song, particularly when Bill was doing an instrumental break, Charlie often got "excited" and began to increase the tempo, thus affecting his timing on making the chord changes for the remainder of the "side."

Why did recording producers allow those types of "takes" to be commercially issued? The recovering post-Depression era was a time when record companies preferred not to make multiple takes of songs unless there was an engineering fault, so the performers usually only had one opportunity to record a song. This was partly the result of record companies scheduling many performers to record on any given day (so studio time was often at a premium), as were the financial costs associated with the preparation and maintenance of wax matrixes then used in the recording process.

It is not always a simple matter to figure out what key certain songs were recorded in. This discrepancy results from how the instruments were tuned at the time of the recording, errors in wax matrix speed transfer to metal disc master for production, etc. Obviously, songs performed in certain keys [e.g., B flat or B natural] would dictate that a capo be used for guitar backup.

In order to adhere to the spirit of the guitar backups used by Charlie Monroe I have chosen the keys that fit best under the fingers for the particular runs and range used in any given song (for instance playing out of G [capo 2] when the song is actually performed in the key of A, as some of the licks played by Charlie Monroe can only be logically played using the G chord shape). I will present numerous backups from each chord family, commenting on the common backup techniques frequently used, as well as any special note sequences, common substitutions and stock backup phrases.

Let's get started!

Charlie and Bill Monroe in the 30's

THE G CHORD FAMILY

Here is a composite backup as used by Charlie Monroe in this song, the very first recorded by The Monroe Brothers on Bluebird Records on February 17, 1936:

My Long Journey Home

The first thing to take note of in this backup is that Charlie Monroe didn't use a standard string band guitar alternating bass pattern, e.g., Root 3 Root 3 or Root 3 Root 5 (R3R3 or R3R5), in the opening measures. Instead he used a 4-beat pattern based on the ascending pentatonic scale, i.e., R365, one frequently used by guitarist Riley Puckett (of Gid Tanner and His Skillet Lickers fame). As you can see Monroe used this note sequence in four of the eight measures of the backup: measures one, two, five and eight. We will see later that he often used this particular pattern in tandem with the G triad (R35) to create a "3 against 4" feel.

The third measure in this song should have been harmonized by the C chord and in the fourth measure by the G chord; however, Monroe got mixed up and usually played a full measure of G played in the third measure followed by a 2-beat C chord and 2-beat G chord in the following measure. In this particular recording he got off to a bad start in his backup and really never caught up with brother Bill, instrumentally speaking; of course, he was somewhat distracted because he was also singing lead vocal at the same time. As noted earlier, that problem was complicated by the fact the Charlie Monroe had a natural tendency to play faster as the song went along (this is true of many of the 60 "sides" recorded by The Monroe Brothers), so his reaction time occasionally suffered as the song progressed.

In this particular backup Charlie Monroe used the standard single beat walkup bass line to establish each chord change, i.e., to the IV chord, to the V chord, and at the V-I cadential figure, using the more conventional R3R alternating bass note approach to the walkup figures themselves.

The eighth note pair sequence positioned on the second beat of the fourth measure (IV to I change) is actually based on the pentatonic scale; Monroe simply abbreviated it by playing the Major Sixth to the Fifth (E to D), then immediately playing the Root on beat 3 establishing the harmonic reappearance of the G chord. You might have expected him to play a quarter note on the second beat (the third of the C chord, E); however, as that note is a common tone with the sixth scale degree of the G Major scale he "rolls over" to the pentatonic scale instead (well, that is how we look at it today; somehow I doubt that he was thinking along those same theoretical lines). As we will see, that particular note sequence is commonly used by him in songs using the G chord family and occasionally when playing out of other chord families. However, you could also consider that note pair as having a "split personality relationship," i.e., in this case the first note acts as the third of the C chord while the second note of the pair acts as the Fifth of the tonic chord.

The first measure of the cadence at measure 7 for the song "My Long Journey Home" is clearly established, resolving to the Root of the tonic via an ascending walkup bass line. Later on what will change is the note sequence that follows the arrival of the Root (and vice versa).

By using this backup in the key of G major as a working template, and creating a four-measure phrase using the chord progression G, C, D and G (one chord per measure) as used in the song "Nine Pound Hammer Is Too Heavy", we can look at additional ways that Charlie Monroe layered harmonic ideas in his backups:

|| G | C | D | G ||
  I   IV   V   I

V to I Cadence

Since the V to I cadence is the most prominent in Western music let's look at that chord progression first, in this case D to G.

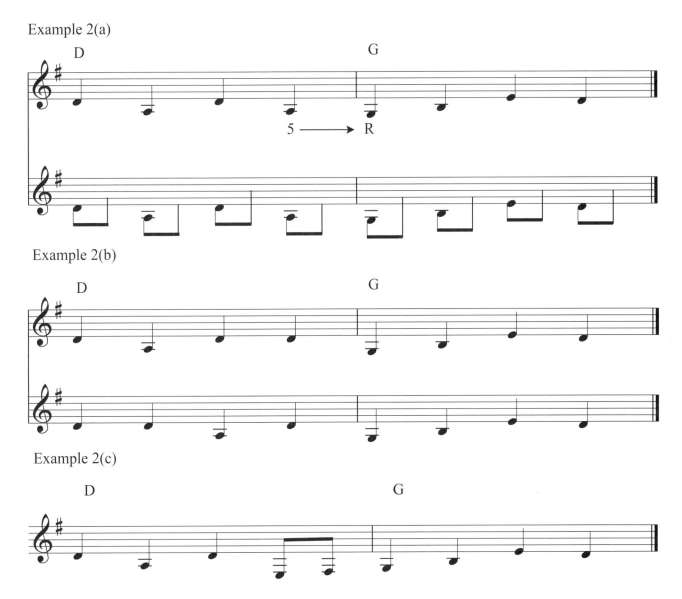

Example 2(a)

Example 2(b)

Example 2(c)

Example (a) demonstrates a basic alternating bass pattern with voice leading from the fifth of the D chord down one whole step to the Root of the G chord (I have also included a similar example where Monroe used index finger upstrums on the weak beats of each beat); example (b) shows two similar usages ending on with the Root of the D chord that resolves down to the Root of the G chord (in this case the D chord Root is a common tone with the fifth of the G chord); example (c) shows a variation on his "stock D chord note sequence" using the walkup to approach the Root of the tonic G chord.

I to IV Chord Change

Here are several ways that Monroe changes from the G to the C chord in the song "Nine Pound Hammer Is Too Heavy":

Example 3

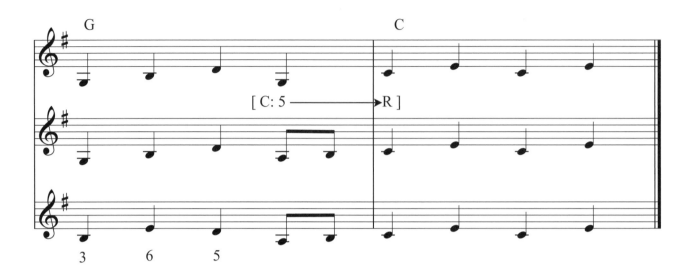

IV to V Chord Change

Since "My Long Journey Home" didn't have a C to D chord change in it, here is a basic example as used in "Nine Pound Hammer…", which is similar to the walkup bass line used to approach the D chord from the G tonic chord:

Example 4

Remember that "split personality relationship" that I referred to earlier? Here is another example of that usage, this time from the C chord to the D chord. However, since the roots of those two chords are a whole note apart it is clear that this eighth note pair is not based on the pentatonic scale, as was the case earlier, i.e., in this instance the first note, E, is the third of the C chord while the A is the fifth of the D chord:

Example 5

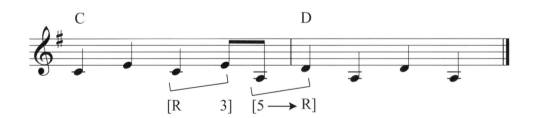

Monroe Pentatonic G Run

At the very beginning of Nine Pound Hammer..., Charlie Monroe plays the following pentatonic lick:

Example 6

I am labeling this note sequence the Monroe G Run to differentiate it from the lick that Bill Monroe was simultaneously developing that would eventually became known as the "(Lester) Flatt G run"; however, Charlie Monroe would not adapt that particular lick in his own backup playing. The Monroe G Run figures prominently in the songs that he plays out of the G chord family (Charlie Monroe occasionally used an upwards strum on beat 4 replacing the low Root of the G chord in that lick).

3 vs. 4 Feel

Charlie Monroe often failed to position the Root of the tonic chord on the downbeat on the first measure of songs. This usually occurred because he was mixing R35 and R365 note sequences in succession creating a 3 vs. 4 feel. Here are two typical examples:

Example 7(a)

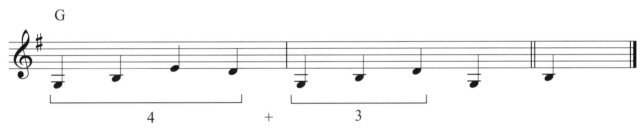

Example 7(b)

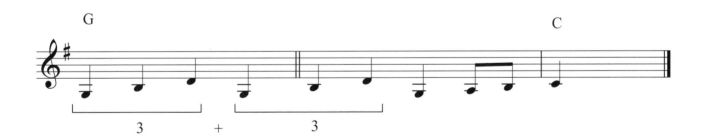

As you can see, those note sequences displace the Root on the downbeat of the verse, chorus or instrumental break; even the Monroe G Run does so because the Root concludes the note sequence on beat 4, thus the third of the G chord is positioned on the following downbeat.

Watermelon Hangin' on that Vine

In this basic composite backup you will once again see use of the R365 chord outline in measures 1, 2 5 and 8, as similarly positioned in "My Long Journey Home". There is also the stock walkup in the G to D chord change; we encounter that "split personality relationship" in the C to G chord change, then end up with the stock V to I chord change that previously outlined.

Monroe plays a couple of interesting variations, e.g., in measures three and four the following note sequences are used:

Example 8

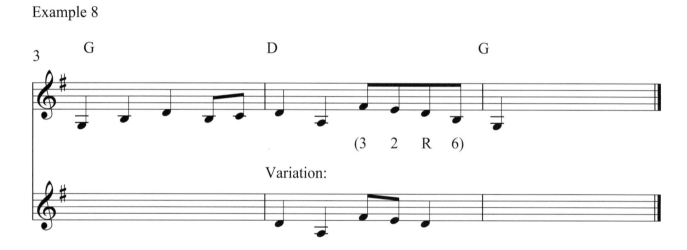

As you can see, Monroe once again used a G chord outline-walking bass line to approach the D chord, then used a descending pentatonic lick for the last two beats of the fourth measure (32R6) that leads back to the G chord (that lick is occasionally varied by not including the sixth scale degree). This is a common lick that Monroe frequently used in the D chord family, as well as some other chord change families that we will see a little later on.

One additional variation that Monroe used in the D to G chord change is based on a Carter Family lick. Note that on the last beat of the D chord he played both the A and D notes (on adjacent strings) as an eighth note pair unit, followed by the R365 note sequence:

Example 9

Do You Call That Religion?

No backup chart is presented for this song. However, three interesting things happen in this song, the first being Monroe's use of the 3 vs. 4 feel once again:

Example 10(a)

Example 10(b)

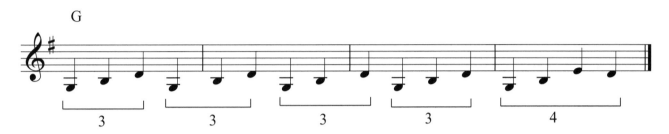

This song uses a 2-beat D chord and 2-beat G chord at the cadence. In this case Monroe decided to position the "Monroe G Run" on beat three of the cadence; the following measure acts as a bridge back to the verse:

Example 11

At the coda Monroe used a glide stroke technique to outline the G chord, a right hand technique that he normally only uses for songs in triple meter:

Example 12

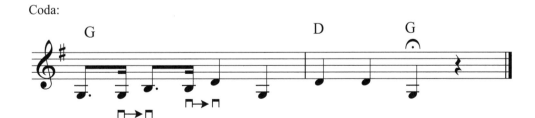

You've Got to Walk That Lonesome Valley

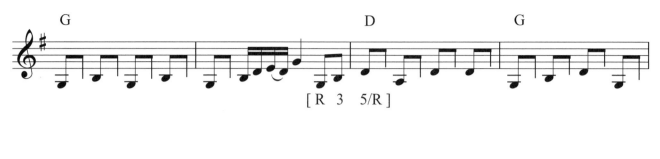

[R   3   5/R]

The first thing you probably noticed was the frequent usage of the Monroe G Run to end virtually each phrase, occasionally using it twice in succession. Let's look at some additional features of this backup, one being that he is using index upstrums on all of the weak beats.

In the first measure Monroe uses an alternating R3 bass pattern, thus setting up the G on the downbeat in the second measure for the Monroe G Run. At the end of the second measure he uses a G triad outline to change from the G to the D chords, i.e., the D note being a common tone between both chords. Monroe frequently uses this technique, or a bass line walkup, for similar changes in his backups for songs using the G chord family.

His transition from the G to C chord at measure 5 is interesting in that the last note is C, not G as expected; this is because that measure in the phrase is usually harmonized by the C chord. Note that when this phrase is repeated again at measure 13 Monroe only changes the octave of the G note on beat three from the third to the sixth string because he is using an alternating bass pattern this time instead of the Monroe G run.

At measure 10 Monroe outlines a G chord outline resulting in the note D being positioned on the following downbeat as the initial note in the Monroe G Run, instead of the Root of the G chord.

Monroe uses two alternating bass patterns for his D chord backup, .i.e., the target note G being approached by either the Root or the fifth of the D chord.

I'm Going [Through]

The backup presented for this song comes from one of the instrumental breaks. As you can see, most of the phrases have been previously covered, e.g., R365 lick, 32R6 D chord lick, etc. Because he began the V-I chord change on the second beat of the seventh measure he had to abbreviate the concluding note sequence accordingly.

One very interesting feature, and one that he seems to use only here in the 60 Bluebird recordings, is his use of a quick hammeron (or slide) to approach the Root of the G chord that is used in this song as a bridge between verses:

Example 13

Vamp:

Of course, this later became a common bluegrass guitar lick.

Will the Circle Be Unbroken

In this backup Monroe uses a new alternating bass pattern in the first two measures. The first measure resembles the R365 pattern in that the first and last notes are the same.

At measure 7 he uses an alternating bass pattern he normally only used when playing out of the D chord family, i.e., the open D to F# on the sixth string (stopped by the left hand thumb).

Monroe surprises us yet again at measure 13 by connecting two triad patterns with a connecting R-3 note sequence (last two beats). This is probably what he meant to do at measure 10 in "You've Got To Walk That Lonesome Valley".

One final thing to make note of is the use of the Monroe G Run in the last measure that is approached by a stock D chord alternating R-5 bass pattern. We will find out why this is significant in the next song.

Roll In My Sweet Baby's Arms

The first unique feature of this backup occurs at measure 3 where Monroe uses successive G notes. In the following measure he uses a descending scale, what I call a 5-R (Five-Root) scale that is used in this instance instead of his stock 32R6 D chord lick. The reason why I call this note sequence the 5-R scale is because the first note of that scale is the fifth note of the G Major scale that descends to the Root, G.

Monroe uses two other note sequences for this G to D chord change at measures 3-4, the first a stock alternating bass pattern, while the second one uses a modified 32R6 lick:

Example 14

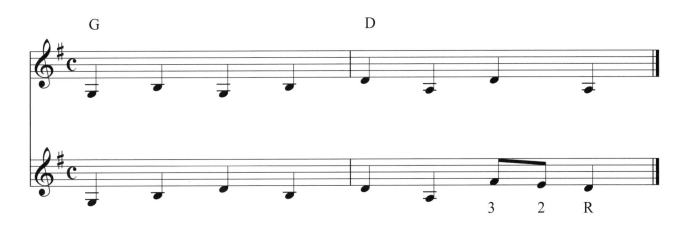

A very important event occurs at measures 7 and 8, as this is the first time on wax that Monroe uses in tandem two licks that he frequently used separately in the earlier recorded sides. From this point on this note sequence would be the one used by Monroe at most V-I cadences when playing out of the G chord family. However, having just said that, Monroe ends the second backup section with the V to I change that he was using earlier, not his new D to G phrase!

Note that when consecutive measures of G to C to D to G chords occur in other songs played out of the G chord family (i.e., the I-IV-V-I chord progression) the note sequences used in measures 5 through 8 of this song are often played by Monroe as stock backup phrases in those other songs.

I Am Ready To Go

In the first backup Monroe uses all stock note sequences. This is followed by a crooked chorus, i.e., 7 measures instead of the standard 8 measure phrase.

At measure 3 in a backup for one of the instrumental breaks Monroe introduces the use of an extra note, G, in the walkup to the D chord (ordinarily he uses a walkup pattern on beat 4 or outlines the G chord, with D being the fifth of G as well as the Root of D, thus a common tone):

Example 15

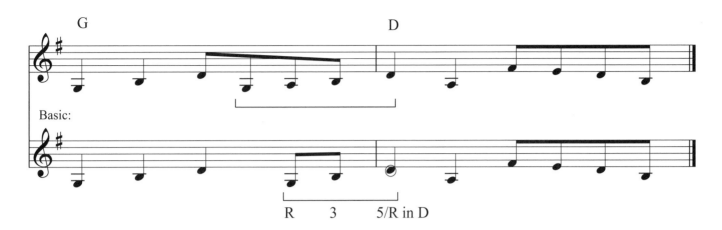

Basic:

R   3   5/R in D

What Would The Profit Be

[5 → R]

5

In the backup to this song Monroe uses all stock phrases, so no backup chart is provided here.

Arkansas Cottonpickers

I Have Found the Way

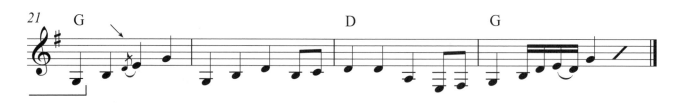

The backups to the verse and chorus use stock phrases with one exception, and that occurs at measure 3 where Monroe uses the 5-6 pentatonic note sequence to approach the Root of the D chord instead of a standard bass line walkup. Since the note on beat 3 at measure 3 is B he couldn't use that note again to begin the walkup, so he chose A to B as the eighth note pair instead.

The backup to the instrumental break is fairly stock. Monroe once again used the 5-R scale instead of the 32R6 lick at measure 4. The principal change to make note of occurs at measure 5 where he used a Carter Family-like quick hammeron in the G chord outline creating a pentatonic note sequence (this is sort of a variation on his standard G Run lick). Also note that he concludes this particular backup with an index finger strum vs. the low G note he normally uses in his G Run.

I Am Going That Way

The backup to the instrumental break has several interesting features in it. The first occurs in the first measure where, once again, Monroe uses a quick hammeron on the fourth string imitating that usage in the G chord just discussed in the song "I Have Found The Way".

At the conclusion of the Monroe G Run in measure 2 he used a bass run to the G on the following downbeat instead of using that standard low G note on beat 4 of the Run itself.

In measures 5 and 6 Monroe features the use of a special pentatonic note sequence.

Kate Cline

This is a fairly stock backup except for the Carter Family-style quick hammeron used in measure 6. As a variation for the opening measure Monroe used hammerons to outline the G chord, this time including the use of a hammeron to the third of the G chord:

Example 16

Roll On, Buddy

This backup contains some interesting variations. The first occurs in measures 3 and 5 where the C chord is outlined instead of using an alternating bass pattern. In the first instance the C triad is outlined while in the second instance an accented passing tone, D, is positioned on beat 2.

In measure 6 Monroe once again uses a Carter Family adjacent string lick outlining a descending G chord; this time he also uses the same technique at measure 14. We saw a similar example of this in the song "Watermelon Hangin' On That Vine" when he outlined a D chord.

The remaining feature to discuss is the use of an enclosure in measure 10 leading to the C chord, i.e., the D should resolve to the C but is interrupted by playing the leading tone, B, on the upbeat of beat 4.

Monroe uses his classic D to G chord run to conclude this phrase.

Oh, Hide You in the Blood

Monroe used a new D chord alternating bass pattern in measure 4 of this backup.

Two new things happen in measure 6. First, Monroe outlined the G triad, then, instead of using the standard B to C eighth note sequence bass run to the D chord, he played just the third of the G chord, B.

On My Way to Glory

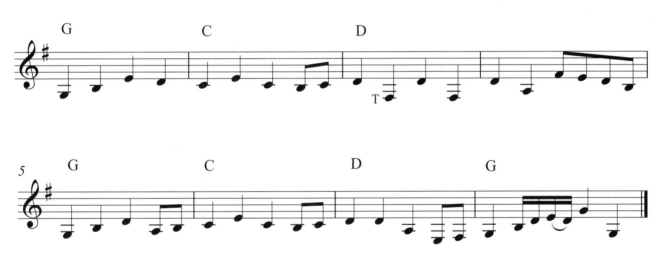

This is another stock backup with the exception of measure 3 where Monroe once again used the low F# as part of the D alternating bass pattern.

He Will Set Your Fields On Fire

This song uses all stock backup changes so the backup chart is not included here.

The Old Man's Story

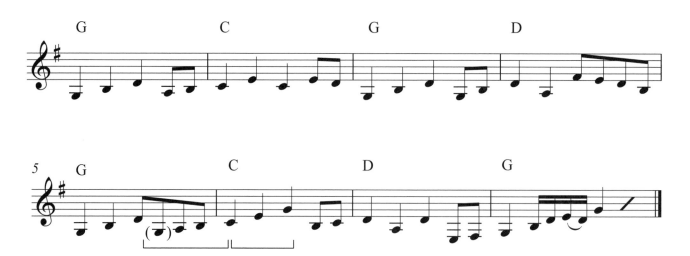

This backup is fairly stock with the exception of Monroe occasionally using the G in the bass line, e.g., leading to the C chord in measure 6. Once again, note the use of outlining the C triad in measure 7 instead of using an alternating bass pattern.

Monroe slightly deviates here from his stock D to G chord phrase that concludes the section in that the second and third beats in measure 7 are reversed, i.e., A to D instead of D to A.

Little Joe

At measure 3 in this stock arrangement Monroe once again had to change the alternating bass pattern before the walkup bass line from the G to the D chord in order to avoid playing the third of the G chord twice in succession, thus he repeats the G note instead.

Monroe also alters measures 5 and 6 in the following manner:

Example 17

You can see that in measure 6 of this variation he does not lay out the G chord on beat 3, but goes directly from the C chord to the D chord in measure 7, no doubt a memory lapse.

A Beautiful Life and On My Way Back Home

In the song "A Beautiful Life" Monroe uses stock changes throughout (this is a rare instance where Bill Monroe doesn't play a mandolin solo once the song begins). Stock changes are also used in the song "On My Way Back Home".

Possum Hunters
from Left, Dr. Bate, Staley Walton, Oscar Stone, James Hart, Walter Liggett and Oscar Albright

When Our Lord Shall Come Again

This is the final song in Common time using the G chord family, recorded at Session 6. Again, right off the bat, you will see numerous uses of the Monroe G Run on the even-numbered measures, as well as index finger upbeat chord strums on the off-beats.

On beat 4 in measures 3 and 7 Monroe repeats the D note instead of using the third of the G chord to approach the Monroe G Run. While he reverted to his earlier V – I chord change to end the introduction, he didn't use his stock change to end this particular break.

Let's now move on to the F chord family.

THE F CHORD FAMILY

On Some Foggy Mountain Top

Charlie Monroe introduces many new licks when using the F chord family. The following come from the song "On Some Foggy Mountain Top":

Example 18

The first thing to make note of is Monroe's use of the 5-6 pentatonic note sequence approach to the Root of the F chord, then the R653 pattern on the downbeat; however, he doesn't conclude that pattern on the low F on the sixth string as might be expected but reverted to the octave note on the fourth string.

Measure 2 introduces a new chromatic lick, R to 3 to flatted 3 to 2 to Root (R 3 b3 2 R). In measure 3 yet another new lick is introduced, Root to flatted Seventh to the Sixth to the Fifth (R b7 6 5). Note the alternating bass in the concluding C chord between the Root and the fifth, instead of between the Root and the third, E.

Charlie Monroe isn't done yet! As a substitute for the chromatic lick in measure 3 he also used a bebop jazz type of line, Root to Major Seventh to Flatted Seventh to the Sixth to the Fifth (R 7 b7 6 5):

Example 19

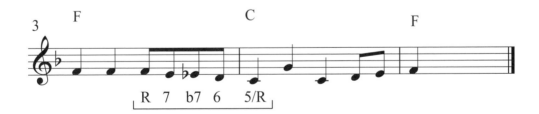

In My Dear Old Southern Home

In this backup you will notice that the Root of the F chord alternates with the third on the adjacent open fifth string (occasionally he will reverse the pattern, i.e., A to F). Once again the C-G alternating bass pattern is used in measure 3 of each phrase section. When the B flat chord appears at measure 6 Monroe simply outlines the notes of the triad; also note the 5-6 note sequence targeting the Root of the F chord at the end of measure 8.

Monroe used the same chromatic licks in the instrumental break that are virtually identical with those used in the song "On Some Foggy Mountain Top".

This World Is Not My Home

While no backup chart is provided for this two-chord song, the I and V chords feature chord tones positioned on every other beat, i.e., beats 1 and 3, with index finger chord brushes on beats 2 and 4. Also, the Root of the F chord is often approached by the third and fifth note sequence in between verses, acting as a bridge:

Example 20

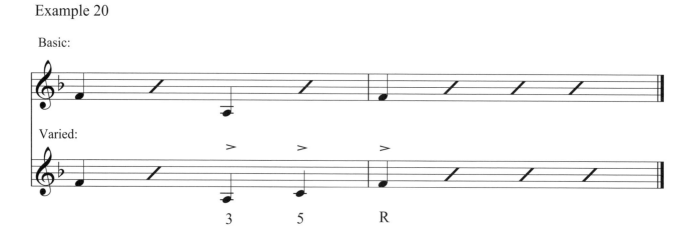

God Holds the Future in His Hands

(5 6 R)

This song only uses the tonic and dominant chords; once again, note the use of upward index chord strums on the upbeats.

In the first measure the Root of the tonic chord is played three times in succession; in measure 4 the fifth of the C chord on the sixth string is used instead of the open third string in the alternating bass pattern. In measure 7 the Roots of the F and C chords are also repeated.

I noted earlier that Monroe often alternated between the Root and the third of the F chord on the fifth string; however, in measure 9 of this arrangement he alternates between the Root and the fifth (on the fifth string).

A new chromatic lick is introduced in this song at measure 12: from the Root to the second to the augmented second to the third (R 2 +2 3) followed by a three-note bass line walkup approach to the F chord. Although the first three notes of this chromatic lick became associated with the Flatt G Run Charlie Monroe didn't use it in his G Run.

The 56 R note sequence can also be found embedded in measure 14.

My Savior's Train

In this song yet another new chromatic note sequence is introduced in measure 3 that includes the flatted sixth (R b7 6 b6 5/R). This is a variation on the lick found in measure 6, by shifting the flatted seventh over one half-beat.

You should also make note of the fact that Charlie Monroe also played the Root of the F chord four times in succession in measure 9.

The Old Cross Road

As you can see the verse uses basic alternating bass patterns with index finger strums on the upbeats.

The first two measures of the break feature embedded 5-6 note sequences. In measure 3 an unusual octave leap of the fifth of the C chord occurs on beats 3 and 4; the R b7 6 5 chromatic lick is used at measure 6. The index upbrush is where you could consider positioning the Major Seventh to create additional chromaticism at that point (similar to that found in measure 2 of the instrumental break backup), or you could shift the flatted Seventh over one beat and use the flatted Sixth on the upbeat of beat 4, as done in "My Savior's Train".

The Saints Go Marching In

As you can see from this backup, all of the phrases are fairly stock in nature, including the use of the R b7 6 b6 5/R chromatic note sequence at measure 3. However, Monroe does employ a couple of variations. At measure 3 he omits the use the flatted sixth and uses the R b7 6 chromatic line instead:

Example 21

In the transition of the I to the IV chord Monroe used an enclosure figure instead of an ascending bass line figure:

Example 22

From northern Alabama, Alton and Rabon, the Delmore brothers

Weeping Willow Tree

The final song in the F chord family in Common time features the rare use of a descending scale line, from F down to C in measure 3.

The backup for the instrumental break features several special note sequences! The first measure uses an unusual alternating F bass pattern followed in the next measure by use of the supertonic on beat 3, disguised as what initially appears to be a 5-R scale in the key of C; however, in this case there was no chord change!

In measure 4 a descending C triad is used with an unaccented passing tone on the upbeat of beat 2.

In measure 6 of the break we encounter a 5-R scale note sequence in the I-IV chord change that in turn leads to yet another special note sequence in measure 7 (based on the C pentatonic scale).

Let's now move on to the D chord family.

THE D CHORD FAMILY

New River Train

The backup for this song opens up with the R653 R lick that we encountered in the F chord family; in fact, Monroe uses it twice in succession in this arrangement. Measure 3 finds the chromatic R b7 6 5/R lick, also used in the F chord family.

In the second measure of the instrumental break the R 3 b3 2 R chromatic lick is used, while in measure 3 of the break the rhythm of the R b7 6 5 lick is varied as quarter note values instead of the usual eighth note values; the same holds true for the ascending bass line at the V to I final cadence.

Paul Warmack & the Gully Jumpers
from left; Burt Hutcherson, Roy Hardison, Charlie Arrington, Paul Warmack

I'll Live On

Break #2

The backup for this song uses many of the same stock licks as used in the F chord family. However, because the key of D is being used the alternating bass for the tonic chord often alternates between the D on the open fourth string and the F# on the sixth string (stopped by the left hand thumb).

Lester Flatt

Sinner You Better Get Ready

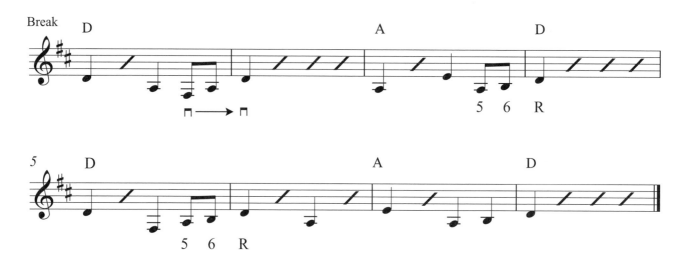

In measure 1 of this break a glide stroke can be used to approach the Root of the D chord on the downbeat of measure 2.

The only notable variation Charlie Monroe uses is at measure 5 where he adds the fifth of the D chord on beat 3, thus shifting the F# to the weak beat:

Example 23

Have A Feast Here Tonight

This is a stock backup arrangement with the exception of Monroe using the R635 lick in measure 3 that in turn leads to the R b7 6 b6 5/R chromatic lick on beat 3. In fact, he uses the R653 lick three times in eight measures!

Rollin' On

The principal feature of this backup is that Monroe outlined the D triad, including the octave note, in measures 2, 3 and 4.

Let's move on to the C chord family where we will encounter several Carter Family-style licks.

The Carter Family

THE C CHORD FAMILY

Darling Corey

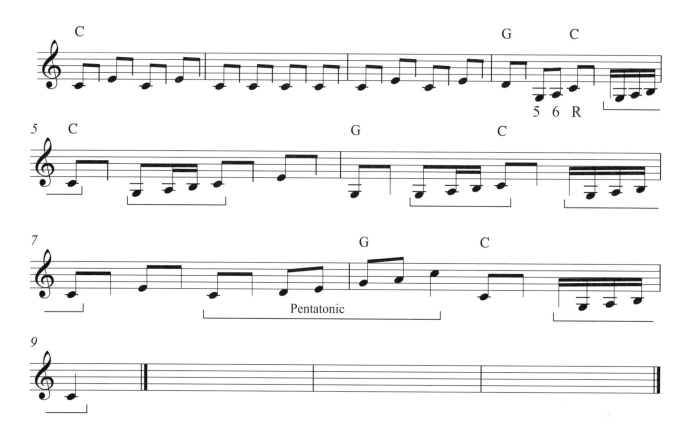

This is a song important in the playing of Bill Monroe as it was the first "side" waxed where he played at the conclusion of this song what would later be referred to as the Lester Flatt G Run. For more information on this please see my book **Old-Time Country Guitar Backup Basics**, specifically pages 51-52. As noted earlier, brother Charlie maintained the use of his own pentatonic G Run in his backups but only when playing out of the G chord family; however, Bill consistently transposed his "G run" in songs arranged in different keys.

The main feature of this particular backup is the use of the walkup bass line from G to C that occurs in measures 4, 5 6 and 8. These lines are all embedded in C chord lines and, as you can see, use faster rhythms.

Monroe also uses a C pentatonic scale in measures 7 and 8 that crosses the bar line.

Here are a couple of other ways that Charlie Monroe plays the first two measures of this backup:

Example 24(a)

Example 24(b)

Where Is My Sailor Boy?

Monroe once again features the use of index finger strums on the upbeats in his backup for this song; also, the choice of notes for his alternating bass patterns in the first five measures are interesting. The remainder of the backup used stock lines.

Take note at measure 3 of the break backup where he uses that "split personality relationship" pair of eighth notes that we previously discussed in C to G chord changes in the G chord family; this time the chord change is from F to the C chord. In this case the A to G note sequence could be interpreted as pentatonic notes common to the C scale.

Early Opry String band, the "Fruit Jar Drinkers"

Some Glad Day

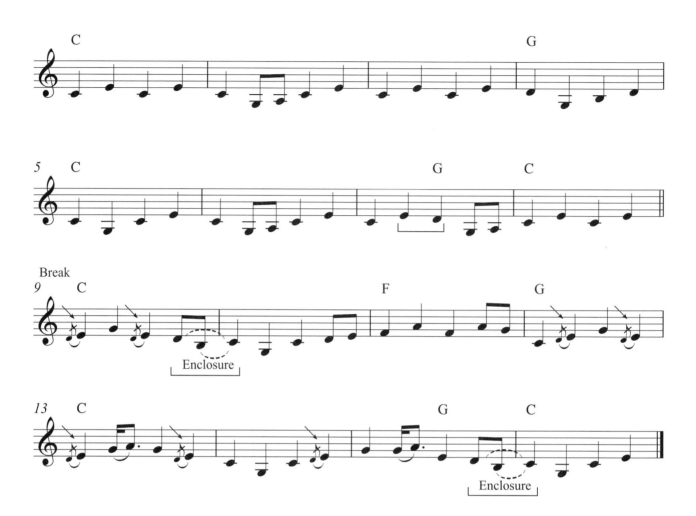

One thing to make note of in the basic backup is the note sequence that occurs in measure 7 where on the third beat the third of the C chord, E, resolves down to D of the G chord. We normally see that note sequence as a pair of eighth notes, i.e., that "split personality relationship" discussed, for example, in "Where Is My Sailor Boy"ßΩ, etc.

The main features of this song are the Carter Family quick hammerons used during the instrumental break for both the C and G chords. Also, make note of the two enclosure figures used at measures 1 and 7.

On That Gospel Ship

The basic backup uses stock lines; however, Monroe occasionally uses the R 2 +2 3 chromatic lick in measure 4:

Example 25

In the song "Mule Skinner Blues", recorded by Bill Monroe and His Blue Grass Boys on Victor records on October 7, 1940, he played a backup lick on his Martin D-28 that is sometimes referred to as a "train shuffle rhythm." This pattern is loosely based on one of the Carter Family licks where four sixteenth notes are played for a single quarter note, i.e., a tremolo. What does this have to do with Charlie Monroe and The Monroe Brothers?

Cunningly, Charlie was able to simulate this shuffle rhythm in the instrumental break with Bill by simply hammering on the note pair in a sixteenth note value while Bill played a steady melodic tremolo behind Charlie. It sounded as if Charlie was doing the complete shuffle rhythm himself on guitar but it is actually a combination of Bill and Charlie's playing.

Here is the backup for that instrumental break:

On That Gospel Ship

Other than the quick hammerons you should make note of the pull off used in measures 2 and 6 in the C chord, as well as the G pentatonic note sequence in measure 7.

Goodbye Maggie

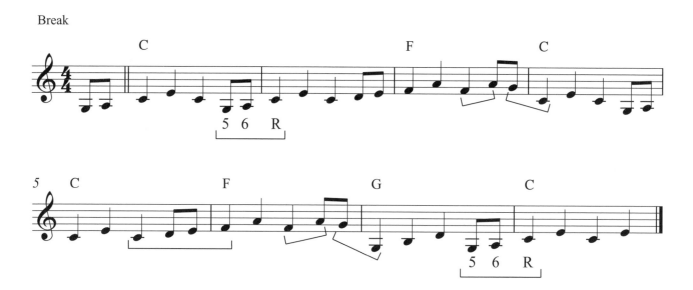

In the backup to the instrumental break presented here note the use of the embedded 5-6 note sequence at the end of the first and fourth measures in C; it is also used at measure 7 in conjunction with the G to C chord change.

Measure 3 once again features that "split personality relationship" note sequence, from F to C. Make note that this same note sequence is used at the end of measure 6 but in the latter case it leads to the G chord instead of the C chord (also note the octave shift between the two G notes).

The final thing to mention is Monroe's use of the standard walkup bass line for the chord change C to the F in measure 5 instead of playing just the third of the C chord, E, on beat 4, continuing the alternating bass pattern.

Pearly Gates

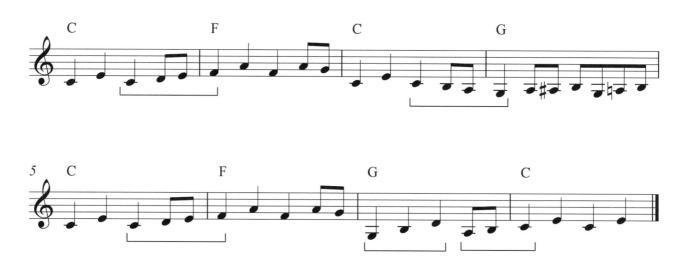

This backup uses stock lines. However, make note of the descending bass line at the end of measure 3 leading to an ascending R 2 +2 3 chromatic lick in the following measure, thus the use of contrary motion.

Let's move on the E chord family.

THE E CHORD FAMILY

On the Banks of the Ohio

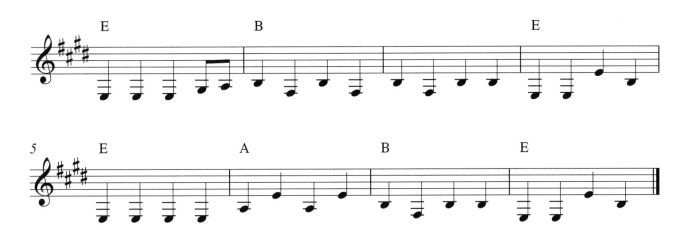

The backup to this traditional string band song is straightforward; however, Monroe varies his basic backup for the IV to V chord change in measure 6 on the fourth beat in two ways:

Example 26

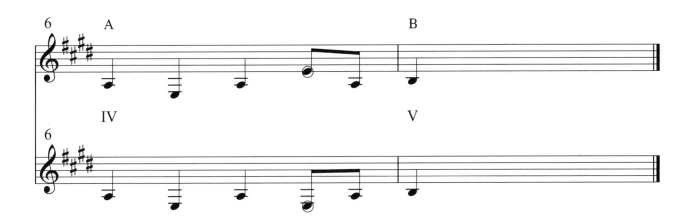

Monroe also used a standard walkup in measure 7 instead of an alternating bass pattern:

Example 27

Now, let's look at the instrumental break:

On the Banks of the Ohio

The R 2 +2 3 chromatic lick is used in two different ways in this backup in measures 1, 2, 3 and 5. In the first measure a descending bass line is used as a "tag" to connect the I to the V chord while in measure 3 an ascending bass line is used to connect the V to the I chord that resolves to the R653 R note sequence; that lick is also used to conclude the break.

Don't Forget Me (Little Darling)

Once again, the basic backup to this song uses familiar note sequences, so let's look at instrumental break backup.

Don't Forget Me (Little Darling)

Break

In measure 2 Monroe used an embedded 56 R note sequence twice in succession; in measure 4 he uses the R 2 +2 3 chromatic lick.

Measure 2 of the break can also be played in the following manner:

Example 28

The chromatic lick in measure 4 can also be replaced by the following standard alternating bass pattern:

Example 29

The last beat of measure 6 of the break features the Carter Family adjacent string lick using both A chord tones that in turn leads to the Root of the B chord; be aware that the E note on beat 4 of measure 6 could also be played on the sixth string instead of stopped on the fourth string, as noted in the previous song "On The Banks Of The Ohio".

Measure 7 contains a special note sequence followed by an unusual rhythmically-varied 5-6 note sequence used twice in succession for the final measure of the break.

THE A CHORD FAMILY

Only one of the 60 songs from the Monroe Brothers body of work is played out of the A chord shape. The song, "Just A Song Of Old Kentucky", is actually played in the key of B natural. Charlie Monroe capos his guitar at the second fret and plays it out of the A chord family. As that song is in ¾ time I will discuss it in the concluding section.

That is it for the songs in Common time. *Let's move on now to the songs in triple meter.*

TRIPLE METER SONGS

Before looking at some of the songs recorded by The Monroe Brothers in triple meter, I thought that it would be interesting to look at a phrase from a song written in that meter as arranged for plectrum guitar taken from a 1932 guitar method. This particular phrase just happens to feature the R365 note sequence that was frequently used by Charlie Monroe in many of his backups in Common time:

Example 30

Waltz fragment (ca. 1932), arranged for guitar

The Glide Stroke

One of the most common techniques used by Charlie Monroe in triple meter songs was to "dress up" the standard "chord note-strum-strum" backup pattern by repeating the initial chord tone at the end of the measure, i.e., rhythmically repositioning it to the final upbeat, then gliding the thumb pick to the next chord tone on the adjacent string in one continuous stroke. The following example shows a schematic diagram of that rhythmic pattern:

Example 31

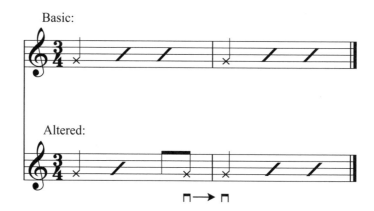

Here are two examples of the glide technique using a C chord; note that the second extract uses all notes of the triad, as used in the song "What Would You Give In Exchange For Your Soul":

Example 32(a)

Example 32(b)

Now, let's look at some of the songs that The Monroe Brothers recorded in triple meter.

Little Red Shoes

Charlie Monroe presents a variety of interesting note sequences in this backup in the key of D Major; as the parts are greater that the whole in this backup I will examine them individually.

First, Monroe used glide strokes from either the fifth of the triad, or the Major Sixth, to the Root of the D chord on the fourth string:

Example 33(a)

Example 33(b)

The glide stroke connecting the fifth to the Root is also used in the triple meter song "I Dreamed I Searched Heaven For You".

Next is an example of how the 568 note sequence can be used to substitute for the 5-R glide stroke just outlined, sans use of the glide stroke:

Example 34

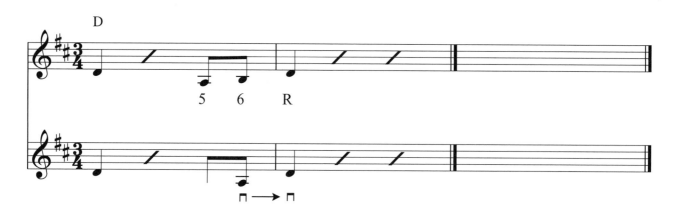

Here is an example of how Charlie Monroe "fit" the R653 note sequence used in Common time into triple meter:

Example 35(a)

Example 35(b)

Next is an example of how the fifth and sixth scale degrees can be used in contrary motion in the same phrase:

Example 36

Here is an interesting example of the R b7 6 5 note sequence in quarter note values (on occasion Monroe repeated the Major Sixth, thus the reason for the second note of the pair bracketed in this example). Note how the note sequence in the first measure was rhythmically altered by Monroe to an eighth note pair:

Example 37(a)

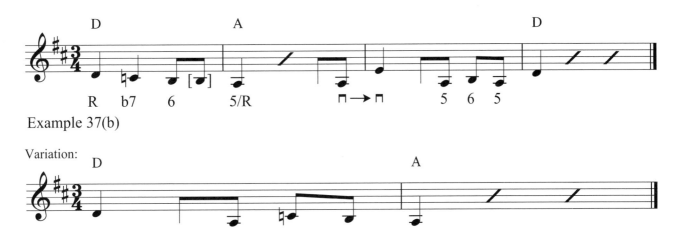

Example 37(b)

Variation:

Also, did you note the pentatonic note lick in measure 3 that led back to the tonic chord? Here is how it evolved in the playing of Charlie Monroe in the context of the V to I chord change:

Example 38

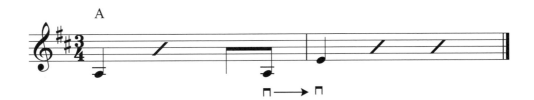

In the dominant key of A, the next available chord tone on the adjacent fourth string is the fifth, E (not the third, C#, which is also located on the fifth string) so the glide stroke connects the Root to the fifth:

Example 39

47

Here is an example of how Monroe uses two licks in tandem with each other in triple meter:

Example 40

R   6   5   R   3   b3   2   R

Drifting Too Far From The Shore

No chart is provided for this backup. However, here is an example of the glide stroke in the context of a I to V chord change that we frequently saw in songs that used the G chord family in Common time. The thing to take note of is that while the G chord is outlined, the last note, D, is a common tone: the Root of the D chord and is the fifth of the G chord.

Example 41

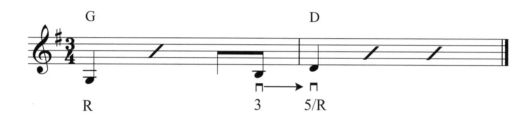

R   3   5/R

The same rhythmic variation for glide strokes can also be used for notes played on the same string, in this case in a I to IV chord change:

Example 42

I Am Thinking Tonight of the Old Folks

Break

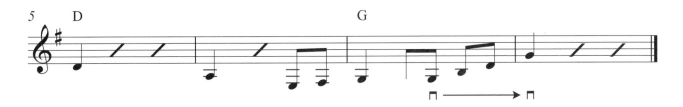

In addition to the standard bass walkup lines used in this backup to the instrumental break note the use of glide strokes on the upbeat of beat 4 at the end of measure 3; in measure 7 three notes are used as part of the glide stroke after the initial G note is played. The latter technique was also used in several songs, e.g., "Do You Call That Religion?", "My Last Moving Day" and "The Forgotten Solider Boy".

Riley Puckett of The Skillet Lickers Band

The Forgotten Soldier Boy

Solo #1:

The main feature of this song is the use of the glide stroke on the G triad to end each section; this note sequence replaces Monroe's use of his pentatonic G Run in triple meter songs. At the end of the second ending note the use of the glide stroke to connect the Root to the third of the G Major chord.

Here is an example of how the R365 pentatonic note sequence beginning at measure 2 of the first solo in "The Forgotten Solider Boy" was adjusted by Monroe "to fit" into triple meter:

Example 43(a)

R   3   6   5

All the Good Times Are Past and Gone

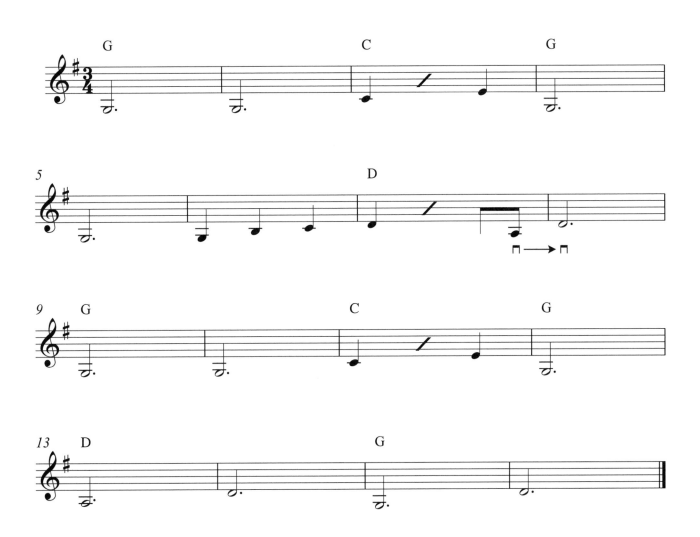

The first thing to take note of in the basic backup occurs in measure 6 where the usual walk up to the D chord is rhythmically altered from eighth notes in Common time to quarter notes in triple meter. Compare the following examples:

Example 44

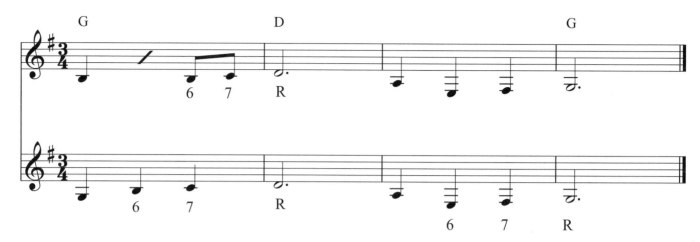

Here are similar examples of this rhythmic variation as used in the songs "I've Still Got Ninety-Nine" and "The Forgotten Soldier Boy":

Example 45

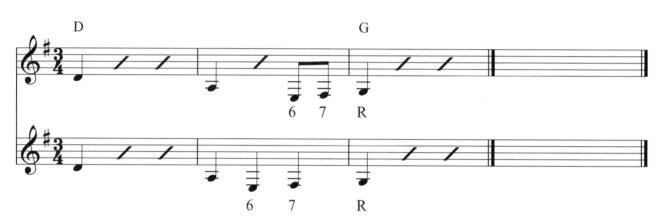

Note the glide stroke usage between the fifth and Root to the D chord at measure 7, i.e., open fifth string to the open fourth string. Monroe also substitutes the following D chord outline for those two measures:

Example 46

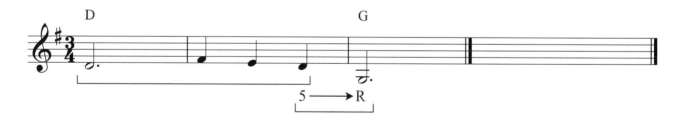

Monroe also occasionally reverses the backup notes in measures 13-14 from A to D, to D to A:

Example 47

All the Good Times Are Passed and Gone

In the instrumental break the opening phrase outlines the Root and third of the G chord that in turn leads to the stock bass line approach to the IV chord, C; a similar approach is used at measure 6 when the Root approaches the V chord, D (in the latter case, the third of the G chord is once again repeated).

Finally, you should make note of the compressed/rhythmically altered G chord in the 14th measure of the break, also used as a substitute for his usual pentatonic G Run in Common time.

The North Carolina Ramblers
left: Posey Rorer, Charlie Poole, Roy Harvey

Let Us Be Lovers Again

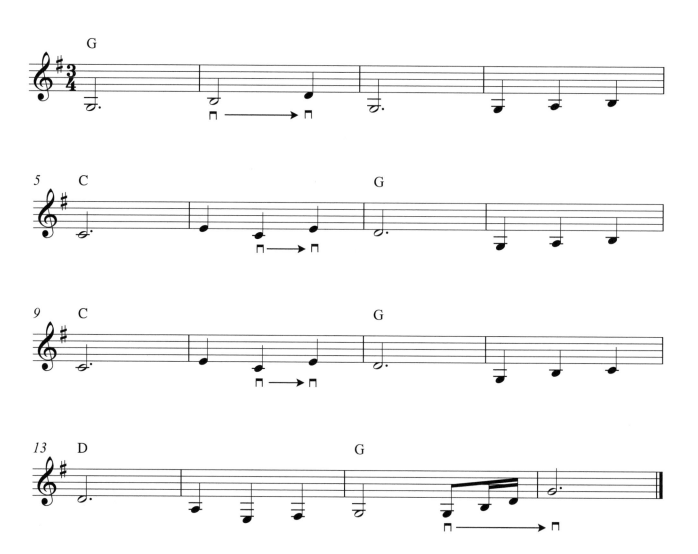

In this backup make note of the G triad that Monroe rhythmically compresses in the 14th measure using the glide stroke.

Here is an example of how the 4-beat G chord outline used in Common time is expanded to take up three measures in this backup:

Example 48(a)

Example 48(b)

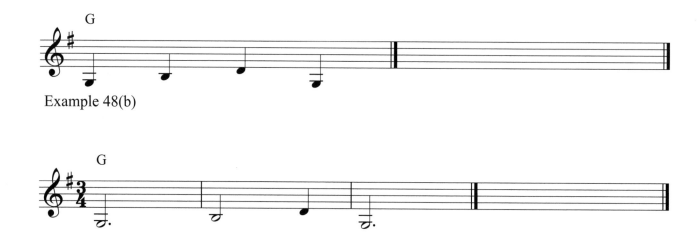

My Last Moving Day

4-Measure Break

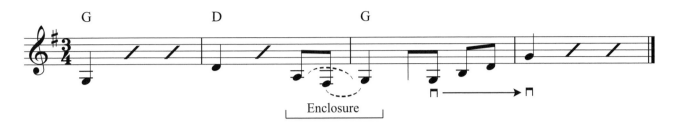

Note that this brief 4-measure break includes use of an enclosure to connect the D to G chord, i.e., the resolution of A to G is interrupted by the leading tone in the G Major scale. A glide stroke is also used on the G triad glide stroke to conclude the phrase instead of the pentatonic G run used in Common time.

I've Still Got Ninety-Nine

I have shown several examples of how Monroe compressed the G triad to simulate his Common time pentatonic G run. Here is a comparison of that lick in Common and triple meter:

Example 49(a)

Common Time:

Example 49(b)

Triple Meter:

Note that in the backup for "I've Still Got Ninety-Nine" that Monroe actually outlines his pentatonic G run in the opening measures.

Six Months Ain't Long

In this backup make note of the descending pentatonic bass line in measure 3 that includes rare usage of the low F on the sixth string, stopped by the left hand thumb (this same note sequence is used to end the second section as well).

In measures 4 and 5 glide strokes are used to outline the F triad.

Measure 1 of the second section features the use of the R 2 +2 3 chromatic note sequence; in conclusion, note the descending pentatonic scale used in measures 15 and 16.

In measure 6 of the first section Monroe occasionally used the following descending note sequence:

Example 50

We Read of a Place That's Called Heaven

Note the use of the embedded pentatonic lick at measures 3 and 15 in the F chord; Charlie Monroe also used it in the song "What Would You Give In Exchange For Your Soul".

Just A Song of Old Kentucky

Introduction:

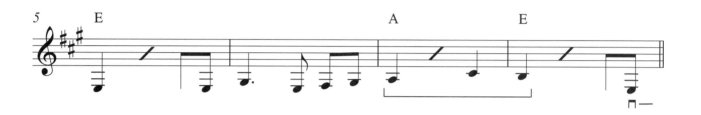

Verse:

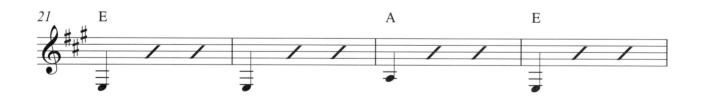

The only backup that Charlie Monroe played out of the A chord family was the song "Just A Song Of Old Kentucky", which was recorded in the key of B, thus he used a capo at the second fret on his original Gibson Jumbo model guitar. Since this song is a staple of Bill Monroe's repertoire, I thought that it would be interesting to layout a longer chart than usual. However, there are only a few note sequences to make particular note of.

Monroe used the R 2 +2 3 chromatic lick in the introduction in measure 3 and in the first section leading to the verse. An unusual alternating bass pattern also appears in measures 7 and 8 of the introduction, i.e., the smooth voice leading from the third of the A chord, C#, to the fifth of the E chord, B, on the downbeat of measure 8.

The final note sequence to make note of occurs at the end of the bridge where the R 2 +2 3 chromatic note sequence is used.

Miscellaneous Techniques.

In cases where the IV chord moves directly to the V chord, the root of the initial chord can ascend directly to the root of the second chord instead of using an eighth note walkup bass line. Examples of this usage can be found in the songs "Drifting Too Far From The Shore" and "I'm Thinking Tonight Of The Old Folks":

Example 51

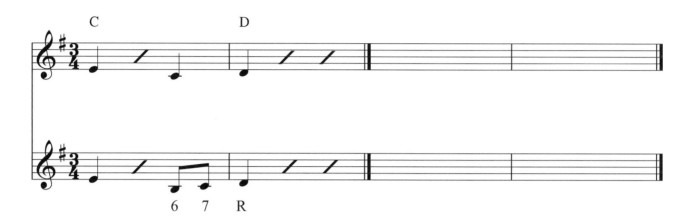

The 5678 note sequence is simply an extension of the 678 note sequence. Here are several examples as found in songs in triple meter:

Example 52(a)

Example 52(b)

In the following example the stock V to I chord change from the G chord family, that Monroe frequently used in his later Bluebird recordings as a cadential figure, is here "converted" rhythmically to triple meter (examples of this usage can be found in the songs "I Am Thinking Tonight Of The Old Folks", "The Forgotten Soldier Boy", and "I've Still Got Ninety-Nine)":

Example 53(a)

Common Time:

Special Note Sequences

Let's conclude by looking at two special "licks" used by Charlie Monroe. The first is based on the 56R pattern but is used in triple meter songs to "fill in the holes" between verses, e.g., "What Would You Give In Exchange"; in fact, he accented each note like a punctuation mark. In addition to this song, Monroe also rhythmically varied that lick, for instance, in the song "I've Read Of A Place":

Example 54

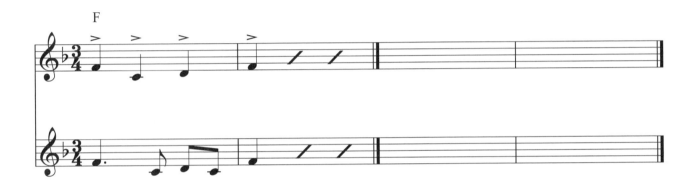

The Blue Sky Boys

61

DISCOGRAPHY

The first three sessions recorded by The Monroe Brothers on Bluebird Records are available on Rounder Records; the complete sessions are available on the Bear Family Records anthology listed below.

Rounder Records
> The Monroe Brothers: What Will You Give In Exchange For Your Soul?
> Rounder Records 82161-1073-2

> The Monroe Brothers: Just A Song Of Old Kentucky
> Rounder Records 82161-1074-2

Bear Family Records
> Blue Moon of Kentucky: Bill Monroe 1936-1949
> BCD 16399 FL

1936 - 1938
Bluebird Recordings
by The Monroe Brothers

RECORDING SESSIONS

Session No. 1
February 17, 1936

My Long Journey Home
What is Home Without Love
What Would You Give In Exchange?
Little Red Shoes
Nine Pound Hammer Is Too Heavy
On Some Foggy Mountain Top
Drifting Too Far From The Shore
In My Dear Old Southern Home
New River Train
This World Is Not My Home

Session No. 2
June 21, 1936

Watermelon Hangin' On That Vine
On The Banks Of The Ohio
Do You Call That Religion?
God Holds The Future In His Hands
You've Got To Walk That Lonesome Valley
Six Months Ain't Long
Just A Song Of Old Kentucky
Don't Forget Me
I'm Going (Through)
Darling Corey

Session No. 3
October 12, 1936

My Savior's Train
I Am Thinking Tonight Of The Old Folks
Dreamed I Searched Heaven For You
The Old Cross Road
The Forgotten Soldier Boy
We Read Of A Place That's Called Heaven
Will The Circle Be Unbroken
The Saints Go Marching In
Roll In My Sweet Baby's Arms
Where is My Sailor Boy

Session No. 4
February 15, 1937

I Am Ready To Go
What Would The Profit Be
Some Glad Day
I Have Found The Way
I Am Going That Way
Kate Cline
Roll On, Buddy
Weeping Willow Tree
I'll Live On
Oh, Hide You In The Blood

Session No. 5
August 3, 1937

What Would You Give In Exchange – Part 2
On That Gospel Ship
What Would You Give In Exchange – Part 3
Let Us Be Lovers Again
All The Good Times Are Passed and Gone
What Would You Give In Exchange – Part 4
On My Way To Glory
My Last Moving Day
He Will Set Your Fields On Fire
Sinner You Better Get Ready

Session No. 6
January 28, 1938

Have A Feast Here Tonight
Goodbye, Maggie
Rollin' On
The Old Man's Story
I've Still Got Ninety-Nine
Little Joe
A Beautiful Life
Pearly Gates
On My Way Back Home
When Our Lord Shall Come Again

CHARLIE MONROE
and the
Dominion Bluegrass Boys
Friday February 8, 1974
7:30 p.m.
Boonesmill Elementary School
BOONESMILL VA.
Sponsored by
The Lions Club
Admission: Adults $2.50   Under 12 $1.00

More Great Guitar Books from Centerstream...